STRAW IN HIS HAIR

A Musical Nativity

By

Ernie Richards

CHARACTERS

Mary

Joseph

Rebecca

John

Nanna

Thieves

3 Shepherds

3 Kings

4 children:

Mark

Joe

Esther

Ruth

Miriam, a neighbour of John and Rebecca

Angel's voice

SYNOPSIS

John and Rebecca, who live in Nazareth, have to go to Bethlehem, like Mary and Joseph, to register for taxation. They sing 'When will our Lord appear?'

Their 4 children, left at home, suspect that their parents are in danger and set out to warn them.

They first meet thieves who try to capture them, but they escape and find shepherds whom they join. They hear an angel singing 'God's going to be a little baby' and they join in.

In Bethlehem at the stable, the 3 kings tell of their travels, their initial rejection of Jesus and then their full acceptance (Kings' song and dance)

The shepherds and the children arrive at the manger.

Mary sings 'Come to Jesus.'

The shepherds give their gifts, followed by the children.

Mary and Joseph sing a bitter-sweet lullaby 'Sweet little baby.'

The children return home, followed later by their parents. Their parents have been shocked by Herod killing all the babies. At first, the children think that Jesus has been killed, but Miriam a neighbour says that Mary and Joseph have fled the country.

In relief they all sing <u>'In the hands of God'</u>, and as the finale they all sing <u>'Noel'</u>.

THE SONGS

STRAW IN HIS HAIR

The scene is a house in Nazareth, about the time of the birth of Jesus.

The children rush on to the stage. The boys are tossing the girl's dolls between them, the girls trying to get them back.

MARK   Catch. Lovely.

JOE   Back to me.

RUTH   Give it to me. It's mine.

MARK   Finders keepers.

RUTH   Mum gave her to me – she's mine.

MARK   Oh, cry baby. Are you missing your little baby? There, there diddums does nobody love you?

ESTHER   Oh u-u- give her back. You've no right to have her.

MARK   How cares about rights? I'm stronger than you, I just take what I want, right?

RUTH   Don't drop her. Don't throw her on the floor.

MARK   She's only rags and scraps. Look – you can tread on her.

He goes as if to tread on her doll.

RUTH   Oh, oh, ow – stop it, stop it, stop it. I hate you – she's mine, she's mine.

The boys taunt her still. Enter Nanna

NANNA   Now now, stop this instantly. Give your sisters their dolls back – <u>now.</u> You should be ashamed of yourselves. I turn my back for 5 minutes and you're scrapping like urchins.

RUTH & ESTHER   It was their fault. They stole our babies. They're murderers.

NANNA   Sh, sh, now it's all over. Come and sit down with me and settle these stupid quarrels.

         I've got enough to cope with, without you lot upsetting each other. We've got to help each other. Settle down.

ESTHER   Now tell us a story.

NANNA   What about?

ESTHER   A King

NANNA   A good King or a bad King?

JOE   Aren't all kings good? It must be marvellous to be so powerful – everyone has to do what you say.

NANNA   Yes, it must be powerful to be a King, but he has to use his power wisely. If he doesn't, he can do bad things and that would make him a bad King.

JOE   But, with all that money and everything given to him, why would he ever want to do bad things?

NANNA   Some people never have enough. However much they've got they always want more and sometimes that means stealing what you want and sometimes even killing people to get it.

RUTH   Ugh I don't fancy that. Tell us about a good King.

MARK   No, tell us about a bad King – you've not done what I've asked you – off with his head – off with his head.

Father and Mother come in with their neighbour, Miriam.

The children greet Miriam.

JOHN   Children listen, Mother and I have something to tell you.

REBECCA We have to go away for a few days.

RUTH   Can't we come with you?

REBECCA No, no, it's not a holiday. We have to go and register so we can pay our taxes.

ESTHER Why do you have to pay taxes?

JOHN   Everybody pays taxes. And the Roman Emperor says we must.

ESTHER Where do you have to go?

JOHN   Bethlehem, because that's where our family come from.

RUTH   But that's hundreds of miles away.

JOHN   No, no, it's not that far.

RUTH   But father making you and mother go that far, it's cruel.

JOHN   It's the law. And the Romans rule over us, so we have to do it.

ESTHER It's unfair. I don't want you to go. Please, please don't.

JOE   There could be robbers or murderers on the way. You'll be robbed or hurt. I beg you, please don't go.

JOHN   Children — we have to. We'll be together
and lots of other couples will be
travelling to Bethlehem. Miriam will be
travelling with us.

MIRIAM   I'm all alone now and John very kindly
said I could go with him and Rebecca.

JOE   Well, I think it's awful. I'd like to kill the
Romans.

REBECCA Now, that's enough of that. Now promise
to be good children for Nanna — she'll be
looking after you 'till we get back. Nanna
don't take any nonsense from them.

NANNA   Oh dear I wish we were a free nation and
not bound to Roman laws and Roman
customs.

JOHN   I know, I know but what can we do?
Maybe one day, one day, we'll be free —
free to be our own bosses. Free to live
where we like and how we like and
worship how we like. One day, one day —

WHEN WILL OUR LORD APPEAR?

Chorus

When will our Lord appear?
When will we lose our fear?
Must be wait for ever and ever?
When will our Lord appear?

Oh, will he come with thunder and with lightning?
Will the earth quake beneath his feet?
Will the mountains tremble as he passes?
Will the rocks melt with the heat?

Or, will he come so softly in the evening?
Will he come so gently in the night?
Will he come so quietly in the morning?
Silently and out of sight.

Chorus

Oh, will his voice be powerful and compelling?
Will he strike all sinners to the ground?
Will he smite the evil and the wicked?
And make all life end in a shroud?

Or, will he smile so gently in his cradle?
Will he sing so softly to his Dad?
Will he croon so quietly to his mother?
So the world no longer is sad?

Chorus

When will our Lord appear?
When will we lose our fear?
Must be wait for ever and ever?
When, when, when, when, when will our Lord
appear?

REBECCA   We are going to leave before dawn in the
          morning, to get a good start. Well before
          you get up. So, say goodbye now.

They all hug and kiss and say their goodbyes.

MARK   If you have to go, promise to bring us
          something back
JOE   Something rich
ESTHER   Something rare
RUTH   Something wonderful
REBECCA   Get along with you. No promises. Now
          off to bed.

Lights fade.

Lights come up. It is the next night.

ESTHER   Can you sleep?
MARK   No. I'm restless.
ESTHER   I don't like Mum and Dad going all that
          distance. It's only a day since they left
          and I don't like it.
RUTH   Look at the stars.
JOE   They're so bright.
ESTHER   Same old stars.
JOE   That's a new one.

RUTH	Don't be silly – how can it be a new one?
JOE	I tell you it is - I've never seen it before.
ESTHER	Joe – you're slipping. I thought you knew all the stars in the sky. You've often told us about them.
JOE	I do know most of them. And that one I've not seen before. And it's moving.
MARK	Joe – come on, that can't be right.
JOE	I tell you, it is. It's in a different relationship to the ones round it and it's moving.
MARK	It's a shooting star.
ESTHER	That's dangerous.
RUTH	It means trouble.
MARK	It brings death.
RUTH	A shooting star always means death.
ESTHER	Fire, flood, famine, war.
JOE	Wait a minute. It's not shooting – it's moving slowly.
MARK	That's even worse. It's like stalking its prey. It's menacing. I'm afraid.
JOE	I don't understand it. It should move fast, if it moves at all.
MARK	It's worrying. It's biding its time – waiting for the kill.
ESTHER	But who? Where is it going?

JOE	It's going South – towards Jerusalem.
RUTH	And towards Bethlehem.
ESTHER	Mother and Father – they're in danger.
MARK	Something horrible is going to happen to them.
JOE	We must warn them.
ESTHER	How can we and warn them of what? You're being hysterical.
RUTH	We must stop them – make them turn back.
ESTHER	Why? Because of a star?
MARK	History shows that when a star moves it means a disaster. The soldiers – maybe there's an emergency. Robbers, murderers – they'll have to stay overnight and who knows who will be on the road with them, or hiding in the desert to come out at night?
JOE	Right, let's go. Get some clothes together – and we'll need food.

They gather clothes and food

RUTH	What about Nanna? We should tell her what we're doing.

MARK	No, she'd only send after us and stop us. She'll be alright.
JOE	We've got to tell her we're going. We must otherwise she'll be frantic.
MARK	Oh alright. Let's write a note – Dear Nanna, We're going away for a few days on a secret mission. We'll see you soon. DO NOT WORRY. Mark OK now, come on everyone. Let's go – it's going to be exciting.

Lights fade.

Lights come up.

The children are on a hillside.

MARK	We'll have to sleep here. We can't afford an inn.
RUTH	But it's just the bare ground.
JOE	Oh stop complaining snuggle down

The children settle down for the night

MARK	Are you alright?
RUTH	No, the ground's hard.
ESTHER	And I'm cold.

JOE — I can't get warm.

MARK — Oh. Come on, think of Mum and Dad – we are going to be saving them. It's worth a few nights' discomfort.

JOE — Try and sleep.

Each child says night night.

Some thieves start to approach them.

THIEF 1 — What's this?

THIEF 2 — Some kids asleep on the ground.

THIEF 1 — Let's see if they have got any money.

THIEF 2 — Is it worth it – they're only kids.

THIEF 1 — Even kids are worth something - we could get a ransom for them.

THIEF 3 — Are you kidding? They don't look rich to me.

THIEF 1 — They're somebody's kids and we can make that somebody pay.

THIEF 2 — Let's wake them and offer them protection.

THIEF 1 — Hey kids wake up – come to Daddy.

The children wake up startled and exclaiming What's going on, etc

THIEF 1   Now, what are you doing in the middle of nowhere? With no one to protect you?

MARK & ESTHER   We don't need protection – we're grown up.

THIEF 2   Everybody needs protection – come with us and we'll look after you.

MARK & ESTHER   No – leave us alone.

THIEF 1   Now, now – don't be nasty to us. We're here to look after you – make sure you come to no harm. There are some nasty people around who could take advantage of you. So be good children and come along with us.

ALL THE CHILDREN   No

MARK   Girls run <u>now</u>.

The boys throw water in the faces of the gang who curse. The boys chase after the girls.

RUTH   That was horrible – those men were awful.

ESTHER   They were creepy. I don't know what would have happened to us if we'd gone with them.

MARK   We need to look for some safe people to be with.

JOE   But we are miles from anywhere – there's just fields around us.

MARK   Let's look anyway – anything to get away
            from that gang.

They hear the sound of a pipe being played.

JOE   What's that?
MARK   It's a pipe.
RUTH   Who would be playing a pipe in the
            middle of the night?
ESTHER   In the middle of nowhere?

They hear sheep bleating.

JOE   They're shepherds and they're making
            music to cheer themselves up.
RUTH   And to keep warm.
MARK   Let's ask them if we can sit with them.
            They've probably got a fire.
RUTH   Ooh, a fire. How marvellous.

*They come on the shepherds sitting round a fire. One
of them is playing his pipe.*

JOE   Hello. We've just had a big fright and we
            wondered – can we sit with you?

SHEPHERD 1   Of course you can. Come and get
                warm.

JOE   Thank you.

ESTHER   Thank you.

RUTH   You don't know how much we have been scared.

SHEPHERD 2   What are you doing here, by yourselves anyway – it's dangerous.

ESTHER   We've come to warn our parents.

JOE   We saw this star in the sky.

MARK   Moving slowly.

JOE   So we thought – they're in danger. We must warn them.

SHEPHERD 1   Where are they – your parents?

MARK   They had to go to Bethlehem – to register for taxation.

SHEPHERD 2   Why do you think they're in danger? You seem to be in more danger than them.

JOE   Because the star is moving so slowly – that means death.

SHEPHERD 1   Where did you get that idea. It does not mean death. If anything, it means life – new life.

SHEPHERD 2   We've been watching it for days now and it's right over Bethlehem – look,

	you can see it over that hill. We thought of going in to Bethlehem to see what it means.
RUTH & ESTHER	Oh, can we come with you please. We must find our Mum and Dad.
SHEPHERD 1	Of course you can. But I don't know if we should go.

A bright light appears overhead and grows brighter.

Voice off stage sings 1st verse of 'God's going to be a little baby' The Shepherds sing the second verse then the children join them in the rest of the song.

GOD'S GOING TO BE A LITTLE BABY

(As a Calypso.)

God's going to be a little baby,
Tender and mild, a little baby
He's going to rule the whole world,
But he's only going to be a little child.

He's going to be the King of heaven
Powerful and just, the King of heaven,
He's going to rule the universe,
But he's only going to be a little child.

He's going to take our sins away,
Forgiving and kind in every way,
He's going to turn night into day,
But he's only going to be a little child.

He's going to end our strife and fury,
Make of our lives a different story,
Bring us to live with him in glory
But he's only going to be a little child.

ESTHER   Come on - let's go and see where this has
            happened – it <u>is</u> a birth – new life, new
            life.

They go off excitedly.

Lights fade.

*Lights come up. The stable in Bethlehem. Mary, Joseph
and Jesus in his manger.*

The 3 Kings appear and start their song.

KINGS' SONG AND DANCE
(this starts like a rap, then bursts into a fast Jewish dance.)

As the star in the East climbed higher
And shone brighter than any star before,
We knew we must leave our wives and children
And follow it to the furthest shore.

We took food and drink on our camels
For ourselves and the King we would find
Spices, silks, rugs for him to lie on,
Rich furs, heavy cloaks, all damask-lined.

Day by day, night by night we rode on,
Moving on through the rain and the snow,
We dreamed of warm fires in our own homes
And yet we knew that we must go.

At last, here's the court of King Herod
We can rest, we can live like a King
But he says he has heard of no child
Of the star, he knows not a thing.

On again, through the freezing deserts,
On again, we must never look back
Still the star keeps on moving and moving –
Till it stops over a broken-down shack.

No King would be born in a stable
With horses and cows living there
There's only a poorly wrapped baby
No crown, but straw in his hair.

This can't be the King we are looking for
He can't lie in a stable bare.
Sadly, we turn and open the door
And step into the cold night air.

Suddenly the whole street is dancing
Whirling and swirling in a mad snow storm
Men and women, children and animals
Making the whole wide world warm.

All the stars and all the planets
Turn and spin to the new-born King
And we know that this truly is God's son
And we sing and sing and sing and sing.

And we dance with all of the people,
Men and women and the children too
And lift them to the skies in their glory
And dance and dance the whole night through.

As we go back to our own country
Through the cold and wintry snows
We can hear all the children singing
We can feel the dancing in our toes.

As we come to every tiny village
Everyone turns out to see us go
We tell them all about the baby Jesus
Tell them the only way we know.

And we dance with all of the people,
Men and women and the children too
And lift them to the skies in their glory
And dance and dance the whole night through.

The 3 Kings go out.

Enter the shepherds and the children.

ESTHER   Ooh, look at the baby.

RUTH   Why is he in a manger? He has no cot.

JOE   Isn't he gorgeous. Can we come closer?

MARY   Yes, you can. And he is happy here – he doesn't need a cot.

MARK   But he is beautiful. What's his name?

MARY   His name is Jesus.

COME TO JESUS

MARY…

Come to Jesus, come my love,
He will save you all
Come to Jesus, come my love,
He will stop your fall

Come to Jesus, come my dove
He will raise you up
Come to Jesus, come my dove
He will fill your cup.

Come to Jesus, come my dear
For now and ever more
Come to Jesus, come my dear
He is, he is, the core.

Come to Jesus, come my sweet
His love will overflow
Come to Jesus, come my sweet
And share his warmth and glow.

Come to Jesus, come my dear
And share your pain and woe
Come to Jesus, come my dear
His love is yours to show.

RUTH   Can we touch him?

MARY   Yes but be gentle

JOE   He won't let go of my finger. He's gripping it so hard. Look, he's smiling at me.

SHEPHERD 1   Lady, we want to give him a present. But we're only shepherds and don't have much.

MARY   You don't need to give him anything – he's quite content.

SHEPHERD 1   But we must. Here, he'll need to have a drink. Here's my cup.

SHEPHERD 2   And happen he'll need to keep his head warm in these cold winters. Here's my cap.

SHEPHERD 3   And happen he'll need to play as he grows up. So here's a ball he can bounce and throw and play tennis.

MARY   Thank you. You are very kind. I know he will appreciate them all as he grows up.

The children are worried – they haven't got any gifts.

ESTHER   We've got nothing, what can we do?

JOE   Give him something of ours.

RUTH   But they're our precious things. They're ours.

MARK   He's got nothing. We have to do this.

RUTH   Ooh, alright then – he can have my favourite doll.

ESTHER   And he can have mine – here.

JOE   He can have my top. It's special. It's spins a long time.

MARK   Ooh, alright he can have my special soldier – he kills everyone he fights. He's strong and can't be beaten.

MARY   Children, thank you for all your gifts. They are wonderful.

RUTH   What can we do now?

MARY   Just love him, as he will do you.

And remember – he is here forever. Whatever happens he will always be with you.

The children and shepherds start to leave, but stop and listen as Mary and Joseph sing Sleep little baby.

SWEET LITTLE BABY

MARY   Sweet little baby, sleep my dear
Sleep in peace and have no fear
Sweet little baby, sleep my dear
Sweet little baby sleep.

JOSEPH   Blow North wind blow, my darling
Blow North wind, blow
We must learn to weep, my sweeting
Mother's smiles turn to death's greeting.
Blow North wind, blow.

MARY   Sleep little baby, sleep my dear
We will watch over you my dear
Play and laugh and cry with you
Sweet little baby, sleep.

JOSEPH   Blow North wind blow my darling
Blow North wind blow
You must learn to suffer and die
In a cold sepulchre to lie
Blow North wind blow.

MARY   Sleep little baby sleep my dear
         You will wake to rule in glory
         The whole world will sing your story
         Sleep, little baby, sleep.

Lights fade and then come up again.

Back home, the children burst in. Nanna is angry.

NANNA   Where have you been? I've been frantic
         with worry.

ESTHER   Oh Nanna – it was marvellous. We went
         to find Mum and Dad but instead found
         the most wonderful baby.

NANNA   A baby – what are you talking about?

MARK   We followed the star because we
         thought it meant death.

JOE   But then we found shepherds who took
         us with them to Bethlehem.

RUTH   Because an angel had told us where to go
         to find the baby.

NANNA   An angel? What baby?

RUTH   The most beautiful baby – with straw in
         his hair.

NANNA   What?

ESTHER   Oh Nanna you would have loved him. He
         just lay there and we gave him all we
         had.

NANNA   You did what?

RUTH   He needed us. And his mother told us he
         would always be there for us. We feel so
         warm.

John and Rebecca come in, tired out and deeply shocked

REBECCA   Oh, children are we glad to be home. We've had a terrible shock. It's the most awful thing that's ever happened.

JOE   What is it?

REBECCA   Well, we got to Bethlehem and got to our inn. That's where they told us that a woman from Nazareth had just given birth – in a stable. I don't know who it was.

ESTHER   Oh, but we do. We were there and saw her and the baby. She's Mary and he's called Jesus.

REBECCA   What?

RUTH   And she gave us a lock of his hair. Look, it's still got straw in it.

Rebecca breaks down crying.

REBECCA   Oh children it's so horrible. We heard screaming and shouting and we went and looked and –

JOHN   Herod was killing all the babies in Bethlehem. The mothers were hysterical. It was awful.

RUTH   Oh Mother how terrible.

ESTHER   But that means –

JOE   Oh no, they'll have killed Jesus too.

MARK   He could be dead by now. Ooh baby Jesus.

Miriam their neighbour comes in

RUTH   Oh Miriam have you heard? Herod's killed all the babies in Bethlehem.

ESTHER   That means they will have killed Jesus.

MIRIAM   No, no that's not true. They're saying in the market that the soldiers went to the inn and went to the stable, but there was no one there – only the animals. Later, the inn-keeper said that they had fled the country.

JOE   Oh, Jesus has been saved.

RUTH   Oh Mother, we've got our present – the one we asked you for.

MARK   Something rich.

RUTH   Something rare.

ESTHER   Something wonderful.

REBECCA What's that?

RUTH   Jesus's love.

MARK   We feel so warm and content.

ESTHER   Like being in a warm, steaming bath.

RUTH   Like being wrapped in the cosiest blanket
you've every cuddled.

JOE   And feeling safe – like being held in the
hands of God.

IN THE HANDS OF GOD

In the hands of God, we can stretch ourselves
Feel power and strength coming through
We can plan, can move, can empathise
We are new made in the hands of God.

In the hands of God, we have no fear
For his love will power us through
We can fight for the poor and the sick
And those whose joys are few.

For the world is full of sickness and pain
And children growing up all alone
We can give them our love and our help
Because we're safe in the hands of God.

At the end of the day when our life is run
And all our light must go
We can come to rest, to rest
To rest, safe in the hands of God.

NOEL
(quick and light)

Noel, noel, noel
Good news we come to tell
About a baby born today
In a manger in the hay
Whatever could he come to say
Noel, noel, noel.

Noel, noel, noel
The truth we have to tell
He came to save us all from sin,
To show us heaven and take us in
All our souls he came to win.
Noel, noel, noel.

Noel, noel, noel
The truth we have to tell
He is born for to die
In a cold tomb to lie
No more on earth to sigh
Noel, noel, noel.

Noel, noel, noel
God has conquered hell
He has risen from the grave
Freely his own life he gave
Our eternal lives to save
Noel, noel, noel.

BOOKS BY ERNIE RICHARDS

Celebrating Shakespeare
An anthology of some of the best of Shakespeare – speeches, scenes, sonnets and songs, together with an introduction, plus notes on every piece. The aim is to encourage everyone to speak these words aloud and share in the joy that Shakespeare's language brings us.

Shakespeare's Women in Love
A look at how Shakespeare presents the women in his plays. His position is not only that women are the equal of men, but he shows that they are superior to men in many aspects.

Blake's Jerusalem
The story of how *Jerusalem* came to be England's unofficial national anthem and the Women's Institute song: inspiring words by William Blake (1807) and thrilling music by Sir Hubert Parry (1915).

Makers of the Women's Institute
This book gives profiles of six fascinating pioneers in the WI movement: Adelaide Hoodless, Madge Watt, Lady Denman, Grace Hadow, Lady Brunner and Cecily McCall. All have a different but wonderful story to tell.

Resolution
This book lists people and events in WI history and in the social history of this country – books, speeches, resolutions and actions – that helped make life- changing improvements to the lives of women and their families.

I won't send roses
Poems trivial and serious, romantic and realistic, spanning a lifetime. The aim is to encourage everyone to write their own poems

A Song for Christmas
Songs for and about Christmas, from a range of sources, mainly from a nativity play and a musical based on *A Christmas Carol* by Charles Dickens.

Straw in his hair
A nativity play based on 4 children's experiences at the time of Christ's birth. It involves them going to Bethlehem, greeting the new birth in the company of the shepherds and returning home transformed by the experience.

A Christmas Carol
Musical based on the novel by Dickens. All these songs arise naturally out of the marvellous language of the famous Dickens' story. They involve happiness, sadness, despair and transformation.

All books available from Amazon

Published by Ernie Richards, Springwood, Church Lane, Sparham, Norwich NR9 5PP   01362 688543

ernierich@hotmail.com

Cover design: Martin Richards

Printed in Great Britain
by Amazon

42999427R00030